IN H

Allaster Adams

Beacon Hill Press of Kansas City
Kansas City, Missouri

Copyright 1999
by Beacon Hill Press of Kansas City

ISBN 083-411-7711

Printed in the
United States of America

Cover Design: Michael Walsh

Library of Congress Cataloging-in-Publication Data

Adams, Allaster.
    In her heart / Allaster Adams.
      p.   cm.
    ISBN 0-8341-1771-1 (pbk.)
    1. Mothers—Prayer-books and devotions—English.   2. Bible—Quotations.   I. Title
  BV4847.A33   1999
  242'.6431—dc21   99-18661
                                                                CIP

10   9   8   7   6   5   4   3   2   1

Dedicated to my mother,
Beryl Adams,
missionary to Brazil

Introduction

I thank you, High God
—you're breathtaking!
Body and soul,
I am marvelously made!
I worship in adoration
—what a creation!
You know me inside and out,
you know every bone in my body;
You know exactly how I was made,
bit by bit,
how I was sculpted from nothing
into something.
Like an open book,
you watched me grow
from conception
to birth;
all the stages of my life were spread out before you,
The days of my life all prepared
before I'd even lived
one day.

Psalm 139:14-16, TM

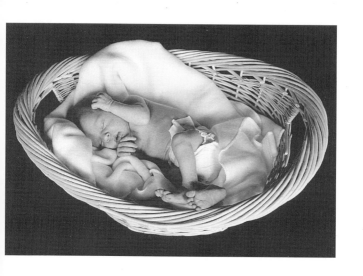

For you created my inmost being;

You knit me together in my mother's womb.

Psalm 139:13, NIV

For we brought nothing into this world,

and it is certain we can carry nothing out.

1 Timothy 6:7

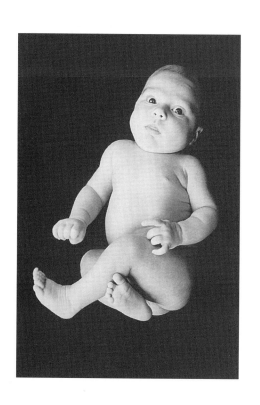

That which is born of the flesh is flesh;
and that which is born of the Spirit is spirit.

John 3:6

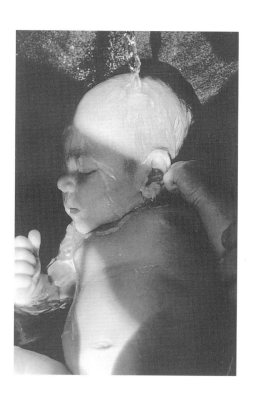

Let everything that has breath
praise the LORD. Praise the LORD.

Psalm 150:6, NIV

Pray without ceasing.

1 Thessalonians 5:17

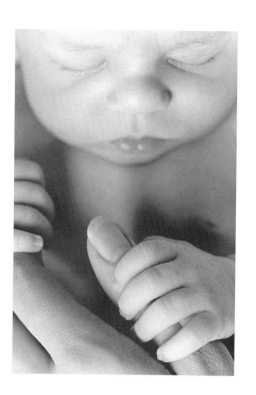

Doth not wisdom cry?

and understanding put forth her voice?

Proverbs 8:1

Verily, verily, I say unto thee,

Except a man be born again,

he cannot see the kingdom of God.

John 3:3

When thou liest down,
thou shalt not be afraid:
yea, thou shalt lie down,
and thy sleep shall be sweet.

Proverbs 3:24

"Before a word is on my tongue

you know it . . ."

Psalm 139:4

I can do all things through Christ
which strengtheneth me.

Philippians 4:13

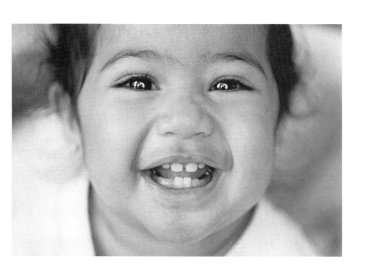

Open thou mine eyes, that I may behold

wondrous things.

Psalm 119:18

One generation shall praise thy works

to another.

Psalm 145:4

The secret things

belong unto the Lord our God:

but those things which are revealed

belong unto us and to our children for ever.

Deuteronomy 29:29

Imprimé en France sur Presse Offset par

BRODARD & TAUPIN

GROUPE CPI

8264 – La Flèche (Sarthe), le 01-08-2001
Dépôt légal : avril 2001

POCKET – 12, avenue d'Italie - 75627 Paris cedex 13
Tél. : 01.44.16.05.00